TONY ASTON

'We Were There' ...and other wartime poems

An Anthology of Original Wartime Compositions

First edition published in paperback 2026

ISBN 978-1-0369-7109-0

A catalogue reference for this book is available from the British Library

Cover design by Tony Aston
Cover image generated by Dola
Illustrations generated by Dola

Published by Big Dog Publishing

Also by Tony Aston

Non-fiction

Redditch – From the Chip Shop to the Batchley
The Bomber and the Weathervane
The Last School Bell

Fiction

Hanukkah to Hell

By Eddie Aston, Tony Aston and Pauline Aston

Non-fiction

This Is How It Was

FOR MY BROTHER, PETER
THE BEST OF SIBLINGS

CONTENTS PAGE

THE COLD WAR

THE FALKLANDS WAR

PREFACE

I penned the poem, “We Were There,” in 2025 when it appeared in my book, “The Last School Bell”. Since then, I have written a collection of war-related compositions which I have drawn together to create this anthology.

The poems mainly surround the First and Second World Wars although I also touch on the later Cold War and Falklands War.

Poetry is something which, until recently, I had never really considered writing but, reading through those contained herein, I am quite pleased with the results. I hope that you will be too! Maybe poetry writing will form part of some future projects, in addition to my other historic and fictional offerings.

War is a topic that has attracted many fine poets over the years. Siegfried Sassoon, Robert Graves, John McCrae and Dylan Thomas are amongst my favourites although, I hasten to add, my efforts compare very little with those of these great writers!

I have, however, tried to depict some of those events, feelings, aspirations, triumphs and sadnesses which inevitably become integral to all wars. I hope I have gone some way to achieving that.

Tony Aston

March 2026

WORLD WAR I

IT WILL ALL BE OVER BY CHRISTMAS

The finger pointed directly at me
from the posters in cities and towns.
Your country needs you, right here, right now.
Take the King's shilling and get your names down.

The girls will love you in your tunic and cap.
A hero they'll call you, and more.
It will all be over by Christmas, they said.
You'll all be back from the war.

Kitchener beckoned from walls and on doors.
The queue went on forever.
The man with the stripes and the pen just smiled,
as we signed for this global endeavour.

We were in before the ink was dry.
You'll receive a letter and a date.
Training and drill, you understand,
but make sure you don't arrive late.

Brown garb and belts were handed out,
though nothing seemed to fit.
And boots that made our feet red raw.
All to do our bit.

Marching, shooting, bayonets and knives.
We were drilled until we dropped.
We'd need all this to save our lives,
and to counter the threat from the Bosch.

The day came around when we headed to France,
on boats that bounced on the sea.
Don't worry, the captain told us all,
you're just the reserve, you'll see.

We saw a sign pointing to Ypres
though none of us knew how to say it.
We saw the trails of wounded and dead
as we arrived with our shiny new kit.

Our eyes were opened by the sight of the many.
I'd never seen anyone dead.
But not to worry, we thought, keep going,
it will all be over by Christmas, they said.

A whole generation died in that war.
Hundreds of thousands of men.
And yet, in another twenty years or so,
we'd be doing it all again.

September thirty-nine, and too old to fight,
but my son was first in the line.
The man with the stripes and the pen just smiled,
"You'll be back by Christmastime."

Forty years later, I pilgrimaged back
and looked at the graves with a tear.
It will all be over by Christmas, they'd said.
But they never told us what year.

THE STRANGEST CHRISTMAS DAY

Christmas Eve and the silence was eerie,
the guns and shells hushed and soundless.
Our first Noel in the trenches of France,
though hopes of peace had been groundless.

This was far from the norm at the fall of the night,
the vacuum, the silence, the still.
The gloom would usually herald a storm,
of the Hun closing in for a kill.

Then clear as a bell, and out of the dark,
save the stars and the light of the moon,
a voice began singing in German, just one.
We knew not the words, just the tune.

"Stille Nacht, Stille Nacht," more voices joined in
from the enemy trenches out there.
"My God, they're singing carols," I said,
"Silent Night I can hear, I swear."

From one voice grew many, down the lines, left and right,
As hundreds more Germans joined in.
Was this Christmas joy, or simply a trap?
Would the fighting still yet begin?

We started singing in reply to the foe.
If they could do it, so could we.
"Roll Out the Barrels," and "Tipperary" rang out.
Let's call their bluff and see.

The carols and songs went on for some hours,
'til heavy eyes and fatigue crept in.
We had the best night's kip for many a month.
No shells, no guns, no din.

The break of Christmas Day brought a shout
from our lookout, on guard for the night,
"There's a Jerry walking towards us," he cried,
a white flag on his gun was in flight.

The soldier walked forward and stopped in the mist,
a bottle of wine in his hand.
He beckoned for us to join him there
in the middle of no-man's land.

We looked at each other then climbed up the ladders
to see what was happening up top.
Many soldiers were standing there
with chocolate and beer they could swap.

There would be no fighting that Christmas Day.
Even a football match was arranged.
We met Klauss, Helmut and especially Kurt.
Everything that day had changed.

We sang, we ate, we drank, we played,
just like there had never been war.
Until nighttime once again came around,
and we had to go to back with our corps.

We shook their hands, we hugged and smiled,
then headed back to our holes.
This was a Christmas, unique and alone,
embedded and carved in our souls.

Boxing Day erupted with fire
as the Germans opened up on our site.
We fired back with all that we had
and hit them with all of our might.

The whistle blew loud – "Over the Top,"
And we went through the mud and the dirt.
I fired at the figure heading for me,
and realised I'd just struck young Kurt.

The powers that be said never again
would such a close union be had.
But I would never forget that day
when the world didn't seem quite so mad.

After the war I traced the parents
of the boy I'd known as Kurt.
Of the time we had that Christmas Day,
and in their eyes, I saw hurt.

But they bore no trace of malice t'ward me.
They knew it was just the damned war.
They'd lost their boy at the hands of my gun,
but here I was at their door.

"It could have been you that fell in the battle."
They looked at me in new light.
Their tears flowed freely, and so did mine,
as they hugged me so close, and so tight.

LADDERS

They were always there, every corner, every bend,
their bases buried deep in the sludge.
Just eight feet tall, they became the foe,
the road to conflict, and blood.

In the days and weeks leading up to the fight,
soldiers would willingly swap
their place on the rungs for the man stood behind,
instead of going over the top.

Day and night, none would look
at these lengths of wood in the lines.
For they knew that when the whistle was blown,
they would lead just to barbs, and the mines.

Enemy chocolate, and a football game,
seemed a million years away,
as they prepared to climb those wooden slats,
just hours after Christmas Day.

Orders received and officers briefed,
hundreds lined up and waited.
The ladders that uniforms would climb and scale,
leading only to where death was located.

When all was done, and the trenches were empty,
just a few remaining alive.
The ladders would wait for the next batch of troops,
But only those ladders would survive.

WORLD WAR II

WE WERE THERE

When Britain vowed to join the fight,
on the soil, in the air, on the sea,
we were there for the call to take arms,
to help set our brothers free.

In metal tubes we flew and fought,
through lights and exploding flak.
We were there and became some of the many,
who never made it back.

When the skins were wrenched from our tins on the sea
by the wolf packs bursting with ammo
We were there as the waves took total command.
Death awaiting, expectant, below.

On the beaches and along the high cliffs,
in the face of burning lead,
we were there in the red bloody sand.
But we never made the beachhead.

Through Italy, Belgium, France and more,
we fought through day and night.
We were there as Hitler's men
killed thousands of us in the plight.

As victory hovered on the streets of Berlin,
we could only see from beyond.
But we were there in the hearts of our fighting pals,
because nothing could break that bond.

Today, we remain at attention and ready,
our names carved clear in the wood.
And *you* are there for all of us,
because we died for the greater good.

And if what we gave has, in some small way,
contributed to making you free,
we'll be there for you, now and forever,
don't forget us, don't let us just be.

When you read our names inscribed on the wall,
stand for a moment and listen.
Because we are still there, with our stories, and our tales,
and we are more than the names that are written.

You are the future to take our names forward,
such that people never forget
that we were there, we made our mark,
but, sadly, we paid our debt.

THE DESERT

Sand forever crunched on your teeth,
and was always there in your feet.
The desert was never a friend of mine,
as again we were forced to retreat.

Desert Fox, the Marshall Rommel,
had held the whip hand for months.
Pushed us back time and again,
from Libyan and Egyptian fronts.

The heat of the day was beyond all words,
matched only by the cold of the night.
The standard kit we'd all been given
was useless when it came to the fight.

Monty, the man to oppose the Fox,
A soldier born of all Tommy's there.
Spoke to them all as a friend and a father.
As one, we'll prevail, he'd swear.

At El-Alamein, his vow came true,
the Fox was compelled to withdraw.
The win was major and pointed the way
to finally winning this war.

Three more long years of battle and fight,
before the Hun accepted defeat.
And we knew our time on the African front
ensured that we couldn't be beat.

The desert, we learned to love and to hate,
the sand still crunched on our teeth,
but the honour in what we had done and achieved
was a privilege we were proud to bequeath.

D-DAY

'We're going south,' our orders decreed,
though nobody told us why.
Some said the Germans were coming across,
some said we're all going to die.

As we closed in on the coastal towns,
we met many thousands of others.
What on earth could be waiting ahead
for us and all of our brothers?

Rain and wind welcomed us in,
despite being the first days of June.
We were billeted in homes, in barns and in trucks.
We hoped we'd hear something soon.

On the fourth, at dawn, we were briefed by the brass.
We were heading across the sea.
The beaches of Normandy waited ahead,
but they meant nothing to me.

We boarded the ships that night in a storm.
At five o'clock we'd be gone.
But the weatherman said there was much worse to come.
To the storm, the Op would succumb.

Twenty-four hours, Ike told us to wait,
in the hope that the rain would recede.
Five on the fifth was the last chance we had
for the Overlord Op to succeed.

The green light was given, anchors were raised,
we were off to whomever knew what.
Twelve hours it took, the Channel to cross,
a horrible churn in my gut.

Landing craft were lowered and manned,
hundreds of them all around.
We were to be the first on the beach.
If I didn't get shot, I'd be drowned.

Like lambs to the slaughter we jumped from the boats,
in seconds, many were dead.
"Keep moving, don't stop," an officer screamed.
We didn't have time to feel dread.

We were armed to the teeth, such a dead weight,
trying to wade through the waves.
Bullets whistled, shells blew up,
sending many good men to their graves.

I stepped over bodies and kit in the sea,
the water a deep shade of red.
I managed to reach dry land intact.
My God, I thought I'd be dead.

Many hours went by in a flash before
we began to make up some ground.
The enemy fire was dying back,
their guns were making less sound.

Off the beach, our final attack,
the firing suddenly stopped.
We'd made it, we'd conquered the foes in the dunes.
Overwhelmed, to the ground I dropped.

I looked back at the beach and couldn't believe
the vision that greeted my eyes.
Hundreds, perhaps more, of bodies and wounded,
a massive cost for this prize.

But this was just the start for us,
through Europe for months we would fight.
Many would make it, many would not,
before victory came into sight.

But this longest day had provided the key,
a foundation for success.
But I would never forget our day on the beach,
and those lost in the carnage and mess.

THE SERGEANT MAJOR

It was the very first time that most had left home,
once we'd initialled the dotted line,
to defend the land of King and country,
we were all persuaded to sign.

The gates clanged shut at the training camp,
we were in, and the first one we met,
was the upright man with boots like glass,
and eyes that we'd never forget.

"Get into line!" he screamed in our faces,
"You 'orrible bunch of scum.
You're weak, unfit, with no discipline,
but soldiers, I'll make you become."

He marched us ragged and was always there,
shouting and swearing at all.
We hated this man who thought he was God,
until off to our beds we could crawl.

In the dead of the night he would be back,
dragging us all from our pits
"Time for cross-country, NOW, in full kit!"
He scared us out of our wits.

For thirteen weeks the course went on,
but things began to change.
From boys we were becoming very fit men,
almost soldiers, what an exchange!

The Sergeant-Major, we learned to respect,
Some might say, even like.
A father-figure who actually cared,
and whose bark was far worse than his bite.

The passing-out parade took place,
with airs from a military band.
The Sergeant-Major bade us farewell,
and I shook him by the hand.

He had been there before, battled and fought,
in the first great war years prior.
The medals he wore were for courage and nerve,
From the start to the final ceasefire.

So I say to the next recruits that arrive
for training to fight the foe.
You'll hate this man as he makes you sweat blood,
But you'll love him by the time that you go.

DOGFIGHT

Morning mist rolled over the field,
as we sat drinking tea in the mess.
The Spits were ready and set on dispersal,
our stomachs feeling full with the stress.

Papers and books lay quiet on the floor
as gazes were cast to the skies.
We awaited the 'phone and the order to go,
to take the Hun by surprise.

'SCRAMBLE!' – we dashed to climb in our craft,
the Merlins roaring with power.
In seconds we'd left the airfield behind,
this was our time, and our hour.

'BANDITS BELOW,' the WinCo came through.
We dived to make the attack.
'LOOK OUT FOR THE ESCORTS' the radio screamed,
'MAKE SURE YOU'RE WATCHING YOUR BACK!'

Again and again we fired on the bombers.
and watched as a couple went down.
Then back up high for another run,
'til the enemy fighter came round.

I flew up high and spiralled back down,
in an attempt to shake him off.
But he was just as good as me,
and I waited for his guns to cough.

I saw and felt a flash and a bang.
In my mirror I saw him explode.
My number two had taken him out,
that was the end of his road.

Nine young pilots took off that day,
but only six of us made it back.
I was one of the lucky ones,
until the start of the next attack.

I looked around to see who was lost.
I checked on all of the crew,
then realised, with horror and woe,
not there was my number two.

"I saw him go down," said one of the few,
"But didn't see him bale out."
The man who had saved my life up there
was gone, of that no doubt.

I tried to grieve, but the tears wouldn't come.
No time to mourn, this was war.
We'd get a replacement for the one that was gone,
and if he bites the dust, then one more.

It wasn't until the war was won
that I remembered all those we owed.
And reflected how it was I'd survived,
only then did the tears start to flow.

ENIGMA

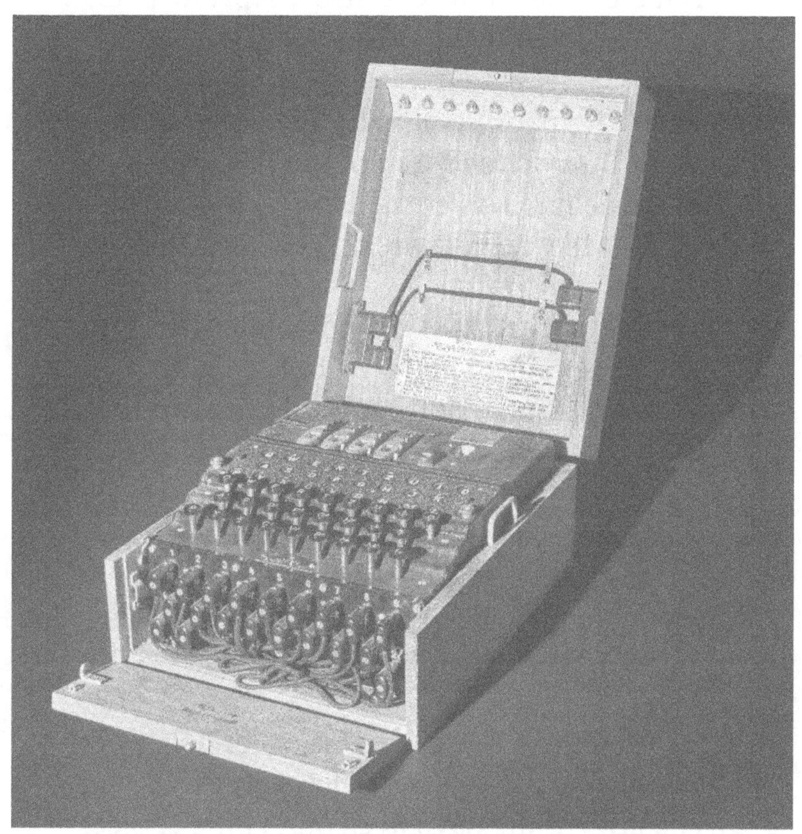

Reams of gibberish, meaningless prose,
spew out from the German machines.
Instructions and orders for U-boats and planes,
But nobody knows what it means.

Mathematicians, tutors and more,
Headed by Turing and Flowers.
A hundred million permutations
to search every twenty-four hours.

Every day the code wasn't found
led to convoys at sea being sunk.
Thousands of hours crying blood, sweat and tears,
To decipher these boxes of junk.

A Soviet spy in the midst didn't help,
said Stalin was on the same side.
But the Reds in the east had a separate plan,
The bomb that the West tried to hide.

The Germans thought Enigma foolproof,
beyond the reach of the British.
But a machine was created to crack a machine,
The Allies would wreak their own Blitz.

Turing constructed a box of his own,
and plugged in the ciphered codes.
Fifteen minutes was all it took
for the open text to unfold.

The war was shortened by several years,
as the Jerry's plans were revealed.
Every move they made, every battle they planned,
Allied victories would yield.

Turing's reward was years of hell
when chemical castration was given.
The laws of the day gave courts little choice.
Being gay was never forgiven.

Decades later, a pardon was granted,
revered for the work he resolved.
The Cambridge professor who helped win the war
by breaking Enigma's hold.

THE NAAFI

Benches and tables lined up in the room,
where hundreds drank tea and ate meals.
Armies march on their stomach, they said,
ready to fight in the fields.

An elderly lady ladled the soup,
though gruel was a better description.
Thinner than tissue when poured in the bowl,
not exactly a hearty prescription.

The main course followed, lukewarm and drab.
Time taken to eat would be brief.
Exactly the same as the evening before,
boiled cabbage, spuds and corned beef.

The men always moaned, the officers groaned,
though nothing would go to waste.
Empty plates were all that left,
but never an inch on the waist.

Apple and custard were served for dessert,
lumpy, sparse and cold.
Little to sustain a man at war.
Little for a spoon to hold.

But the NAAFI was the place to be seen,
to catch up with colleagues and friends.
To talk of what was and what might be again.
God knows when this bloody war ends.

Tomorrow, we'll all be here again,
to speak of success and of grief.
But one thing's for certain and never to change,
It will still be spuds and corned beef!

GRAVES

I saw a grave out there on its own
Bright, in the autumn sun.
A pilot, died in combat flight,
Shot down by an enemy gun.

I saw seven graves all in a line
A Lancaster bomber crew.
Frozen in searchlights and hit by the flak,
Lives snatched, but none of them knew.

I saw a hundred graves in a single field,
all from the same division.
Each mown down on the D-Day beach,
as part of the grand invasion.

A thousand more graves as far as I could see,
row upon row of white stone.
Impossible to imagine these lives, all lost.
Together as one, but uniquely alone.

I looked and saw countless graves.
Foes, lying next to our friends.
All these young men, such a terrible waste.
Did the means really justify the ends?

HOME

Victory in Europe had come and gone,
six long years we'd endured.
Celebrations, parties and flags.
No more bombs, and peace assured.

But there was still a war far away to be won
on the other side of the earth.
The Japanese Empire, a formidable foe.
We'd fight for all we were worth.

Our CO had spoken on the 8th of May
"Don't think you're being released,
there's another job that has to be done.
We're being sent to the Far East."

No chance of leave, more training to come,
war in the jungle was new.
The Japs were experts at what they did.
For us, new skills to accrue.

We sailed on the ships, thousands on board,
to the Cape through the Suez Canal.
Late July came, then everything changed.
Were we not now heading for hell?

At anchor for days, a week, maybe two.
An order to send us back home.
It seems the fight in Japan was done,
something to do with a bomb.

The whole World War was finally over
and back to Blighty we're sent.
Two weeks leave I was now allowed,
a return to my cottage in Kent.

Three bloody years since I last went back home,
a school my daughter had started.
Would she still know me, would she be scared?
Would she even recall we'd been parted?

I knocked on the door, I hadn't a key,
but movement I heard from inside.
A tiny pale face peered out through the crack,
the face of my girl, and I cried.

"You're my Daddy," she said, her face lighting up,
I swept her up in the air.
I hugged and kissed both her and my wife,
Such a special moment to share.

I always knew I would have to go back,
but a date had finally been set.
By the end of the year, I'd be back home for good,
an old life to find and reset.

I never thought I'd see the day,
the end of the army and war.
But family life felt welcome and warm,
behind our cosy front door.

UNLEASHING THE MONSTER

In the mid-Pacific is Tinian Island,
a dot in the sea no one knew.
Enola Gay awaiting the word.
A lifetime job for its crew.

A ball of death strapped under its belly,
the likes could not be perceived.
The Manhattan Project was coming to life.
Who knew what could be achieved?

Skipper Tibbets was the pilot in charge,
to deliver this parcel of carnage.
Six hours in the air the flight would take,
to put paid to the Japanese savage.

The war in the West was already done,
but the East was a raging inferno.
The GI Joes were making no ground,
against the stubborn Mikado.

A different solution had to be found
to prevent losing thousands more soldiers.
Oppenheimer's baby was born,
incalculable weight on his shoulders.

The Gay at thirty thousand feet,
dropped its load with no self-reproach,
then left with maximum turn and speed,
to gain distance from its covert approach.

The light when it happened was blinding and strong.
the blast taking hold of the plane.
But what the crew couldn't see below,
was the bloodshed, the permanent stain.

Seventy thousand died in those seconds,
With countless others to follow.
But still the Nippon failed to give in,
there'd be another bomb to swallow.

Hiroshima and Nagasaki died
in that fateful, awful campaign.
The Japanese ceded, the war was over,
but the bomb never wreaked havoc again.

THE CAMP

We rolled through the gates in our tanks and our jeeps.
The silence was overwhelming.
Skeletal men, many close to death,
huge eyes that were simply staring.

No signs of uniforms, weapons or rank.
Those in control were long gone,
leaving behind humanity broken
and the proof of what they had done

Rumours had spread across the West
of atrocities, cruelty and spite.
But we were not prepared for what we could see,
for the awful, unbelievable sight.

Mountains of bodies, stacked one on another,
lifeless, gassed and decaying.
The pervasive stench of rotting flesh
oozing from where they were laying.

Further inside, we met with the ovens,
many warm, some even still crammed.
Ashes and bones of those now no more,
of humans indiscriminately damned.

We fed those living, though more of them died.
We tended the weak and the sick.
But minds as well as the bodies had failed,
recovery would be anything but quick.

Nuremberg loomed for those deemed to blame,
and many would be facing the rope.
Death would come quickly, not callously, prolonged,
unlike those that they'd killed with no hope.

Auschwitz today commemorates the dead,
together with those who endured.
Spectacles, suitcases, shoes, on show,
their memories forever assured.

BENEATH THE WAVES

Sixteen days since we left the port,
spirits higher than ever.
Our targets, the U-boats, the scourge of the ocean.
Our mission, their power to sever.

Cruising fathoms beneath the ocean rollers,
Atlantic waves overhead.
Seeking the wolf packs lurking below,
those that would see our ships dead.

Our convoys travelled from across the pond
with fuel, munitions and food,
from our friends in Canada and the United States,
to help us prevail in this feud.

Under the water was lonesome and cold,
our safety just two sheets of steel.
The risk of the ocean seeping through cracks,
was ever present and real.

The radio op would cry out aloud
if he heard a blip in his cans.
"BATTLESTATIONS!," the shout would go up,
and we'd slip into well practiced plans.

Our primary aim was to save our ships,
even if it meant that we fell.
Sacrifices might have to be made.
We might have to take a Hun shell.

A blip detected and silence fell,
Then several more, all close together.
There was not just the one, this was part of a pack.
The wolves were starting to gather.

Signals were sent to the ships on the top,
escorts prepared for a clash.
Depth charges readied, coordinates set.
They were closing in like a rash.

Our modern sonars had picked them up,
but theirs were just as good.
Could they hear us, as we spotted them?
What if they could, if they would?

A flash and colossal bang ensued,
as a ship up top took a hit.
The crew on board didn't stand a chance
as the hull exploded and split.

Enemy, a hundred yards ahead,
The radio op declared.
Torpedoes loaded, ranged and primed,
this U-boat would never be spared.

'FIRE ONE,' yelled the skipper above all the noise,
and the missile departed its bunk.
"FIRE TWO," the second followed the first.
Fingers crossed the sub would be sunk.

Seconds passed before we knew
that the first torpedo had missed.
Then a huge explosion made us rock and lurch,
as *their* missile narrowly passed.

A direct strike from our second shell
holed the enemy U-boat's tank.
Its crew would know little of what came next,
the sea gushing in as it sank.

The wolves retreated for another day
The convoy would safely continue,
making port soon after with its crucial loads,
to strengthen the Allies brave sinew.

Again and again the scene would recur
as convoys sailed at great cost.
Until the time when Hitler conceded
that the Atlantic battle was lost.

MEN ON THE GROUND

For hours on end, the groundcrews would wait
for the Hurricanes, Lancs and Spits.
To see if their crews would safely return
from stopping the enemy blitz.

When planes came in, filled with holes or worse,
the men on the ground would pounce.
"We need to get them back in the air,"
No effort spared, not an ounce.

Spanners and drivers, welding and rivets,
all were used for repairing.
Panels replaced, new parts installed,
amid blood, sweat and much swearing.

Mending the planes given the highest import,
getting them ready for flight.
Making them safe for the battle ahead,
whether during the day or the night.

The men on the ground said *they* owned the planes,
Machines that the crews just *borrowed.*
"Please bring them back in one piece," they would plead,
"Try not to increase our workload!"

But work they would, sometimes twenty-four hours,
Such that most of the aircraft could fly.
Then, once again, for hours on end,
The groundcrew would scour the sky.

THE BLITZ

Nine months ago, we heard war was declared,
but nothing over here ensued.
Bomb raid drills and the building of shelters,
But few, if any, attacks from the feud.

All that changed the following year,
when the Jerries quit their Channel traverse.
Hundreds of enemy bombers were sent,
to make our suffering worse.

Cities and towns, airfields and ports
all felt the weight of the loads.
Thousands of civvies, homeless or dead,
the conflict had reached a crossroads.

As well as London being a primary mark,
places were hit country wide.
Coventry's cathedral degraded to ruins,
Plymouth destroyed dockside.

The bombs continued, fifty-six nights,
even Buckingham Palace got hit.
But the Germans failed to take account
of the British morale, so close-knit.

Shops stayed open, businesses worked,
postmen still emptied the mail.
No amount of enemy repression
would cause the British to fail.

Internal squabbling at the Reich highest levels
brought an end to the airborne offensive.
Goering was not the most popular man,
losing most of his planes proved expensive.

Three more years of battle would pass
before the Bosch shot again from the sky.
Their scientists inventing something brand new.
A victory from rockets they'd try.

First the V1, a pilotless bomb,
thousands of the missiles were sent.
Once out of fuel over England's fair land,
they'd fall, bad luck where they went.

Weapons got better and the Germans were buoyed
by a rocket that travelled through space.
V2 was born, a formidable shell,
that could fly through the air without trace.

But all the time, through occupied land,
our forces were winning their fights.
Before very long no more missiles were launched,
no more trembling and terror at night.

When the war was over in forty-five,
the mess left behind was dire.
Countless killed, home and abroad,
all affected, every town, every shire.

But Britain prevailed, rebuilt and reborn,
in the years that followed the war.
Our resolve and morale had won the day,
and it would continue to soar.

SURVIVOR

For hundreds of years I've been standing tall,
watching everything coming and going.
Born from a fire, vicious and strong,
Then seeing a great city growing.

The crowning glory of my designer, Wren,
was the dome to which many would flock.
For miles around I'd be admired by all,
from Hyde Park to St Katherine's Dock.

Kings and Queens have walked through my doors,
Nelson and Wellington buried.
In later days Charles and Diana
would walk down the aisle to get married.

In nineteen-forty all hell broke loose,
as the Nazis attempted to master.
Heinkels and Dorniers swirled overhead,
the strikes became stronger and faster.

I watched from above as missiles rained down,
taking buildings and people alike.
Massive fires blazing all round,
like the past returning to life.

The attacks continued for week after week,
but our boys were up for the fight.
A famous photo was taken of me,
With searchlights piercing the night.

After the war came a plan to rebuild.
This could have been centuries prior.
Rubble and carnage removed from the ground
for buildings, built bigger and higher.

A brand-new city arose from the ashes.
With my height I witnessed it all.
But people will still flock to see me again,
for I'm the survivor, the mighty St Pauls.

THE LEADER

When war was declared in thirty-nine,
views in the House were divided.
Chamberlain's *parlé* with the Fuhrer had failed.
Members believed his visit misguided.

Halifax fought for instant appeasement.
"Do a deal with the Nazis," he roared,
"Give the Germans the land that they want,
or our country will be put to the sword."

For over a decade, Churchill had warned
'bout the build-up of Germanic arms.
How it had overrun lands all around,
he tried hard to raise the alarm.

But few of those in the House really listened
to this man with a tainted repute.
A drunkard, they said, deluded and old,
but a man that no-one could mute.

A no-confidence vote was laid to the floor,
for Chamberlain, a most bitter pill.
It became a straightforward choice for the House,
Halifax, or belligerent Churchill.

Though disliked by many, including the King,
Winston was assigned to the helm.
But Halifax relied on the House turning down
the Premier's plans for the Realm.

"We'll fight them on the beaches," he said,
"In the fields and on the seas"
"We shall never surrender" was his final call,
"We will not be brought to our knees."

Order papers were waved and thrown,
Halifax shrank in his seat.
The country supported this cigar-toting man,
who vowed we would never be beat.

Times would be tough and many men lost
before Winston declared us the winners
of this awful war across the globe,
and the end of the Nazi Berliners.

Churchill was knighted, and forever revered,
As the man who ensured our freedom.
The right man, in the right place, the right time,
My God, how badly we'd needed him.

He lived his life for twenty more years
until, at ninety, he was gone.
A state funeral, the Queen decreed,
With salutes from many a gun.

The likes of Winston will never again
appear as the head of our land.
He was one of a kind, exceptional, unique,
but with the common man he would stand.

EQUAL

I’d never in my life held a riveting gun,
nor a wrench or a hammer to be true.
My world until now had been housework and stove,
Until to the war I gave you.

Hundreds of thousands of men joined up
leaving factories and workshops depleted.
A threat to fighting the enemy abroad,
a risk to the job being completed.

What could be done, the call went out.
Millions of us could unite.
But “women?,” they said with a sigh or a sneer,
“What could they ever bring to the fight?”

But unite we did, in the factories and more.
We toiled, we laboured, we sweated.
We would never let anyone scoff and then tell us,
that we were just an object to be petted.

We made bullets, packed shells, built rifles and guns,
welded and hammered and drilled.
We made sure we sent them their planes, tanks, and ships.
Fewer of our men would be killed.

But once the day in the factory was done,
we had another role to discharge.
We still had families and houses to mind,
and there was no-one else to take charge.

So meals would be cooked and children fed,
before a few hours' sleep we would take.
We prayed that the bombers would miss out our street,
that tonight they would give us a break.

Our thoughts as the Germans flew overhead,
sighted by Hurricanes and Spits,
that it was all the bullets and shells that ***we*** made,
That was putting an end to the blitz.

Before we knew it, the sun would come up
and it began all over again.
Back to our benches we would drag ourselves
daily 'til whoever knew when.

In May forty-five it came to an end,
and our men began to come back.
But jobs they would all be looking to find.
The future for us ladies looked black.

Many of us were laid off our work,
to cater for all of the vets.
Discarded like fag ends on cold rainy days,
No-one knew what would come next.

My friends and I had all been there,
when the country was in need of our strength.
But has-beens and surplus we had now become.
Once again kept at arms-length.

Twenty-odd years would pass us all by,
all of us greyer and older.
Until something stirred in the hearts of our young,
something new, intense, something bolder.

Women's Lib were the words on their lips,
equality for all demanded.
Bras burned in public, demos and marches,
radicals and rebels they were branded.

The Suffragettes provided a model
from their claim for the vote years before.
The women of the sixties were coming of age,
The underclass they would be no more.

It would still take many more long years
before women were seen as less sinister.
But who'd have believed that, in seventy-nine,
There'd be a lady Prime Minister.

My thoughts go back to those days in the war,
and I'm proud of all I was tasked.
With my army of ladies in hairnets and skirts,
We did more than ever we were asked.

And now I'm in the winter of life
and my days are growing shorter.
But I'll always remember that time long ago,
And I've written it all down for my daughter.

THE FIREMAN

I never believed when war broke out,
just how bad the damage could get.
Bombs raining down, night after night,
something I would never forget.

No sooner were fires from the night before
dampened so they couldn't bounce back,
than the daylight faded once again,
and we waited for the next attack.

We were not disappointed, never were they late,
as swarms of bombers appeared.
The explosions, bombs and the fires returned,
became everything we had all feared.

Never likely to douse all the blazes,
too many, we had to make choices.
Then sometimes in silence we had to stand,
on rubble, to listen for voices.

Much of the city was destroyed by the planes,
but you could never say that of the folk.
Everything lost, and nowhere to go,
but they'd still be telling a joke.

Gripping hoses, climbing ladders,
the heat was overpowering.
Buildings collapsed and we had to watch out
for the glass and the bricks that were showering.

Many a time, when our water ran out,
we could do nothing but stand and look,
'til more bowsers came to latch on to hoses,
but masses of time that took.

Attacks in waves for four or five hours,
there was little that any could do.
Many in shelters awaiting all clear,
praying that they'd see it all through.

When it was over the people came out
as the flames we were striving to douse.
Sometimes, it was us that had to show them
a crater, where once stood their house.

In time the city would build and repair,
but now was just ruin and carnage.
Our role would again be lasting all night,
to limit devastation and damage.

Back home for breakfast we'd eventually go,
whatever the time of the day.
Now and again, for some of us,
that home had been blasted away.

Me and my colleagues seemed omnipresent,
though really thin we were spread.
Our lives on the line every hour of the shift,
buckets of sweat we would shed.

But I never wanted to change my job,
despite the perils and dangers.
This was me, doing my bit
for my country, my friends and for strangers.

THE HOME GUARD

The Forties began, invasion risk high,
protection of our Isles became key.
The Local Defence Force became a creation,
to halt an approach 'cross the sea.

Men from the first war, too old for service,
Boys out of school, still too green.
Thousands came forward to protect their homeland,
in their lines, proud to be seen.

Pitchforks and stakes were all that they had
for the first few months of the year.
But nothing deterred these brave local men
from defending that which they held dear.

A change of name, No.10 decided,
The Home Guard would be its new title.
Training in everything needed would follow
for its role which was seen as so vital.

They soon became known most affectionately,
by the folk in the towns and outside,
as Dad's Army, they would now be referred,
and the name bonded, far and wide.

Most were employed, had jobs in the day,
to and from work they would go.
But every evening, with uniforms donned,
Presence on the streets they would show.

Before too long, they were given their guns,
Enfield rifles and sidearms.
Attempts to invade or control would be thwarted
by our brave men from banks, shops and farms.

Guarding, observing, reporting, defending,
were parts of Dads Army's job.
Obstruction, delay, harass and protect,
To defy the invasion, no prob!

Unlike the characters today on TV,
these volunteers were professional.
They knew how important their roles to be,
protecting their towns was obsessional.

As things turned out, our Isles stayed safe,
there was never a successful incursion.
But had they arrived, our first line was ready,
to provide the defence and diversion.

At the end of the war, the Home Guard was done,
and a decision made to disband it.
They'd completed their duty, and finished their job,
just as Churchill had planned it.

Every year on Remembrance Day,
they're revered, and thanked, and respected.
For these volunteers would have laid down their lives,
giving far more than was ever expected.

DUNKERQUE

Pinned down on the beach for what seemed like forever,
the Luftwaffe flexing its air power,
Our chances of making it home alive,
diminishing with every hour.

The Jerries with their blitzkrieging style,
had hit Belgium and France at some speed.
Now they were headed to the northern French coast,
for their invasion plans to proceed.

There wasn't a way we could beat them out there,
outflanked, outnumbered, out armed.
Once the French had surrendered, we'd only one choice,
retreat, prevent being harmed.

Our options amounted to only two,
Calais or the Port of Dunkerque.
The former looked about to fall,
and the latter would take some hard work.

The enemy closed as we entered the town.
Street fighting had started to fail.
We headed out for the beach refuge,
hoping we'd live to tell the tale.

Hundreds of thousands amassed on the sands,
the British Expeditionary Force.
But this was it, no further to go.
The end of the line was the shore.

Unbeknown to everyone there,
Churchill had hatched up a line.
Hundreds of boats would sail 'cross La Manche.
He prayed they would make it in time.

He had been our PM just a couple of days,
when the crisis became exposed.
Chances of success were minute,
so many problems were posed.

How many lives of our men could he save?
Best guesses were varied, some barmy.
Twenty thousand, perhaps a few more,
but too few to form a new army.

Still on the beach being attacked from the air,
morale being increasingly blighted.
Until that is, we spotted our ships,
and we all started getting excited.

But how could we possibly all get off
to our ships out there on the sea?
A bleedin' miracle would be needed now,
but what else did we see?

Fishing boats, dinghies, pleasure cruisers, yachts,
hundreds heading our way.
Before too long we were boarding in hoards.
Churchill indeed saved the day.

Despite heavy bombing from the Stukas above,
more than three hundred thousand escaped.
Far greater than people had possibly thought,
Churchill's war reign had clearly been shaped.

We would reform over the coming four years,
before invading north France with our tanks.
D-Day happened in June forty-four,
jointly with Canadians and Yanks.

But this could never have happened at all
without the seamen and the small ships.
We lived to fight so many more days
to prise open the Nazi grip.

THE SPIV

I couldn’t possibly go to war,
bad chest and flat feet they wrote.
Well, the doctor who saw me kind of said that,
once I’d paid him a hundred pound notes.

But I’m doing my bit to keep people happy,
supply and demand, you know.
OK, it’s done sort of furtive and sly,
Don’t want the law to stem my cash flow.

People need something, maybe stockings or fags,
and they’re willing to pay the right cash.
Yes, they have to pay more than they did in the shops,
but it’s always on offer from my stash.

My style of buying is something unique,
making deals with those in the know.
Things might occasionally fall off of a lorry.
It all makes my business grow.

Tax is something akin to a theft,
my hard-earned bread in harm's way.
But I don't want to waste the taxman's time,
so with me, my money will stay.

Much of my work happens at night.
Well, I need my sleep in the day.
Blackout comes round and the lights, they go out,
Makes folk more comfy to pay.

I've been locked in the cells a couple of times,
and I've been asked by the courts, why not serve?
So I slap my doctor's note on the desk.
They asked me that? What a nerve!

Bottles of whisky are favourite for pubs,
their normal supply drying up.
I'm there to assist, whatever the day,
and I generally get a free sup.

My house has been searched a hundred times,
but the law doesn't have any notion.
And I'm not revealing to you today,
my wares and my treasures locations.

I learned years ago the power of cash.
There's few who cannot be bought.
Police, Excise, pub landlords and more,
but none of them want to get caught.

So we have an arrangement, and I keep my mouth shut,
for some extra notes in my jacket.
Well, it wouldn't do if everyone knew
what they did, they just couldn't hack it.

Now and again, one or two owe me,
and I fall a bit short of expenses.
A few broken windows, or a bloody black eye,
soon brings them back to their senses.

So there we are, I'm providing a service.
Without me, folk would have nowt.
I'll be there, whatever they want,
and all they need do is shout.

SAD REFLECTIONS

From one past midnight on the eighth of May,
Churchill said it was done.
We may allow ourselves time to rejoice,
but the war in Europe was won.

Every town filled with delirious people,
six long years it had taken.
Parties for children on streets sprang up,
joy once again reawakened.

But so many servicemen couldn't be there,
and never would be again.
Wives, sons, daughters and kin,
had lost the closest of men.

The war had been fought and finally won
but for some at a terrible cost.
Families were wrenched apart with grief,
so many of their men had been lost.

80 years later on Remembrance Day,
a veteran, a hundred years old,
spoke of our country as it is today,
and of the pup he thought we'd been sold.

Did the sacrifice made by so many back then,
make a nation about which to trumpet?
No, he replied, those awful deaths
and sacrifices were just never worth it.

So many friends he had lost to the war,
believing a better world lay ahead.
But today he looks at the mess all around,
And says we've been badly misled.

He said he thought he was fighting for freedom,
this was what he'd been taught.
But the country today was a more awful place,
than ever the one for which he'd fought.

LEAVING HOME

Our house was safe, my world, my life,
my friends all living nearby.
We played marbles, cricket and hopscotch outside,
No matter the weather, wet or dry

My Dad had left us months ago
To fight for our freedom, Mum said
But little had changed for me or my pals
Apart from the rations of sweets, meat and bread

We still went to school down the road every day,
And walked off to church Sunday morning.
But change was afoot that would affect us all.
And it happened without much warning.

Mum talked to me, said I'd have to leave,
But not for very long she stressed.
My safety was far more important, she said.
But my heart thumped hard in my chest.

I didn't understand what she was talking about.
Where would I go, when, how, and why?
Did she no longer love me or want me?
I clung to her skirt and I cried.

For several days I sobbed and wept,
And my friends were feeling the same.
We would all be sent off for an unwelcome trip,
Tied-on brown labels with our name.

The day arrived and my case was packed,
I screamed and got dragged through the door.
A train awaiting the hundreds of kids,
To whisk them away from the war.

Mum waved a hanky to say goodbye
Before wiping the tears from her eyes
As the engine began to pull us away,
Her feelings she couldn't disguise.

Then she was gone, and the town turned to fields
I felt lonely, cheerless and scary.
Then a nearby voice, small and trembling, spoke up,
"Hello, my name is Mary."

Her eyes were rubbed red, the same as mine,
I'd seen her before at school.
We started chatting, and her fears mirrored mine.
We both thought that life was so cruel.

Several hours passed by before we arrived
at the station where our journey ended.
A lady and clipboard walked smartly across,
Towards me and the girl I'd befriended.

To the Village Hall in line we were marched
The air smelt fresh, just like heaven.
But it would be several strange and long days later
before I accepted I'd arrived in Devon.

I'd never been to the country before.
I'd never even seen a cow.
The farmer's wife who took me in
said she'd teach me how to plough!

I was lucky with the place that became my home
I was looked after and treated well.
But I missed my house and especially my Mum.
In my letters to her I would tell.

Mary was housed a few roads away
And we went to the same school together
We ended up as the best of chums
And pledged our friendship forever.

After several long years, the war was over
and back to our homes we returned.
The bombings had taken so much of the town,
so many old buildings upturned.

Mum looked older and greyer than before.
The conflict had taken its toll.
But Dad would be coming back home again soon.
The family once more would be whole.

Sixty years later, I look back and recall
those days that fashioned my life.
Then I gaze across to the chair next to mine
And thank God I have Mary, my wife.

THE COLD WAR

THE BERLIN WALL

An August evening, the sun going down,
the last night that East would meet West.
Wire with barbed spikes, blocks gaining height,
families split and no longer blessed.

A legacy borne from the end of the war,
Winston had cautioned so sure,
that a curtain of iron had been drawn across.
More pain for the West to endure.

Stalin and Krushchev, from their Moscow desk,
had harboured designs from the start.
Never shared with the Brits or the Yanks,
they kept them close to their heart.

A greater Russia, a Soviet Union,
with many small nations entrapped.
Those from Estonia, Poland and more,
round the hammer and sickle were trapped.

Berlin became slashed, a city in half,
guarded by men and bright lights.
Guns pointing all night and all day,
aiming the crosshairs and sights.

Many tried escape but were killed on the spot,
life extinct there and then.
American uniforms at Checkpoint Charlie,
saw it happen, again and again.

Reagan and Gorbachev took control,
"Open those gates," was the call.
Thousands of people joined in with the throng,
on both sides of the wall.

The Communist decree crumbled and fell,
in the Fall after twenty-eight years.
Once again families would meet,
to kiss, to hug and shed tears.

The city today is vibrant and free,
though parts of the wall still remain,
to remind the world of what went before,
and to see the indelible stain.

THE EXCHANGE

A chilly night, in the damp spring of sixty,
wondering if the others would appear.
The edge of Berlin, we waited, expectant,
a line of armed aid at our rear.

Months it had taken to get to this point,
where our man might come in from the cold.
Covert discussions and deals that were made,
but trust on both sides could unfold.

The Soviet spy was secured in our car.
He was as hopeful as us.
Been in our prison for nigh on a decade,
for acts deemed so treacherous.

For fifteen years he had worked as a Brit,
with access to our secrets and our men.
As a seasoned agent in MI6,
he fooled us time and again.

Year after year he was passing on
confidences, secrets and events.
His masters sitting in their Kremlin tower,
embracing it all with content.

Our man, whom we were hoping to see,
had been no more than a courier.
No notion of the details locked up in his case,
his role just to take and deliver.

He'd been betrayed and, as he drove through the East,
the Commies had enacted their plan.
Taken at gun point, his day was done,
the Stasi had captured their man.

So here we all were as midnight approached,
waiting for things to evolve.
Would the Russians keep their word and turn up?
Or might all our plans just dissolve?

A word as the wire crackled to life,
and we saw them arrive in the dark.
On the other side of the Bridge of Spies
we watched as they slowed up to park.

I opened the door of my car and got out,
the prisoner walking beside me.
The same was happening ahead of us,
two figures, but too distant to see.

The four of us closed in towards the middle,
and I saw it was indeed our man.
We waited, still yards short of each other,
for the signals, part of the plan.

The signs were made, and instructions given,
to both internees on the road.
Then the two of them walked forward and passed,
both heading for a safer abode.

No words were exchanged, no niceties held.
We were back to our cars and away.
But this exchange likely one of several,
and we'd be back here again someday.

THE FALKLANDS WAR

GOTCHA!

In early April of eighty-two,
by way of shock and surprise,
the island of Georgia in the Antarctic seas
was taken as an Argentine prize.

Our brave Marines fought back with valour,
but numbers had overwhelmed them.
Galtieri's men had sprung into action,
the Malvinas their targeted gem.

For many years, in Argentine eyes,
The Falklands was part of their land.
Hundreds of years had befallen since
they were colonised by British hand.

The islands and seas of the group were consumed
in the days after Georgia was taken.
But Thatcher was having no part of that,
her islands would not be forsaken.

A Task Force was quickly amassed and dispatched,
with several of our aircraft carriers.
Control of the air would be vitally needed,
the task for our coveted Harriers.

Beneath the waves our subs were set,
protecting the exclusion zone.
No enemy vessels were allowed inside,
any trying would be sunk like a stone.

Thirty days on, intelligence confirmed
the Belgrano threatening, no doubt.
A light cruiser ship with a thousand men,
but inside the zone, or out?

The decision was Maggie's, and hers alone.
Might the ship turnabout, open fire?
The risk was too great, her mind was made up.
The threat not allowed to grow higher.

Urgent signals Conqueror received,
our nuclear sub standing by.
Take the ship out, the order was given,
buttons pressed in the blink of an eye.

The Belgrano became engulfed in flames,
unable to remain afloat.
Men were seen to jump overboard,
but only the Press would gloat.

"GOTCHA!" the headline the following day,
although many hundreds had died.
But no-one on the Conqueror cheered,
no smiling, no sense of pride.

Years of debate, discussion and talk
would follow this wartime op.
And even today, the question is asked,
was the Belgrano inside, or not?

www.ingramcontent.com/pod-product-compliance
Lightning Source LLC
LaVergne TN
LVHW081320110826
845149LV00006B/1555

9781036971090